A
Glimpse of
DARTMOOR
VILLAGES

John Risdon

Peninsula
Press

Photographs by the author.

The map of Dartmoor on pages 16-17 is reproduced with the kind
permission of the Dartmoor National Park Authority.

Published by Peninsula Press Ltd
P.O. Box 31
Newton Abbot
Devon TQ12 5XH

Tel: 01803 875875

© Peninsula Press Ltd 1992
Reprinted 1997

Printed in England by Kingfisher Print & Design Ltd, Totnes, Devon.

ISBN 1 872640 06 0

A GLIMPSE OF DARTMOOR
· VILLAGES ·

Contents

Buckland-in-the-Moor

Introduction

The following pages are intended as a brief introduction to twelve villages, or, in two instances, hamlets, that can be found within the Dartmoor National Park. It is a glimpse, a sample of what Dartmoor has to offer the visitor.

The villages cover a wide spectrum of Dartmoor's history and culture and all are unique in what they have to offer. Each one can be enjoyed at a glimpse, or, if preferred, delved into in greater depth. In either case finding the unexpected can give you the greatest satisfaction.

In the majority of cases Dartmoor's villages are of considerable age, and stone, timber and slate have weathered harmoniously into the surrounding landscape.

For those who wish to escape the multitude, commercialism and candyfloss for a while, these villages can offer a tranquillity and appreciation of all things beautiful, with man and nature working in harmony.

An additional bonus will be the country and moorland lanes with their vistas and hidden depths; lanes that have to be explored in order to reach the villages, as the majority are not on major highways.

To help you find your way, each village has an Ordnance Survey (O.S.) Landranger Map sheet number and map reference. All the villages can also be found on the O.S.Tourist Map of Dartmoor or the O.S.Leisure Map of Dartmoor.

In conclusion, may I wish you an enjoyable visit to the village(s) of your choice and PLEASE, may I respectfully remind you that every village, every house, every farm, is somebody's home; please treat it as though it was yours. THANK YOU on their behalf.

The Author

Born and bred in Devon, and with a career spanning the worlds of education and book-selling, John Risdon, has over 40 years, gained an intimate knowledge of an area which in his own words, has become part of his very being, developed through the soles of his feet, and the senses of sight, sound and feeling, together with the learned words of those like-minded Dartmoor folk that he has been lucky enough to spend time with.

◆

Gidleigh

Situation: O.S.Landranger Sheet No.191, map ref.671884
Services: Telephone box only.
Nearest town:.Chagford.

In its isolated position, high up on the edge of the North Moor, the settlement of Gidleigh is rather more a hamlet than a village. Yet it is the centre of a widespread rural community. The less than half-a-dozen cottages that are situated near the little church of the Holy Trinity certainly define that fact. Also, in that the Post Office and Youth Hostel (shown on all O.S. maps) are no longer functioning at the time of writing, one could be misled into thinking that the community here no longer existed. However one would be wrong, and the use and upkeep of church and village hall indicate just how active is the wider community centred on Gidleigh. Look carefully and the signs are apparent, from the beautiful state of the interior of the 16th century church to the beech tree trunk notice board.

Beside the church are the remains of Gidleigh Castle. The castle was a fortified manor house in the 13th century, the medieval administrative and ecclesiastical centre of the whole parish of Gidleigh. Both church and castle are blanketed in a bed of rich tree growth and curtained behind lichen and fern covered walls.

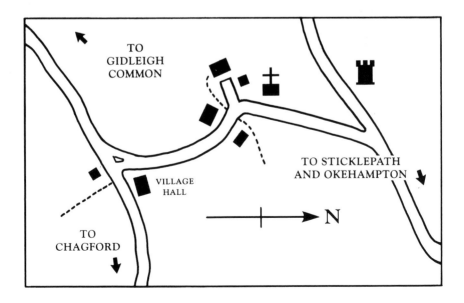

Notice Board at Gidleigh

It is possible to visit this beautiful place and see no one. Peering through the ageing iron gates of the castle, it is easy to imagine that you are the first visitor for a hundred years.

Holne

Situation: O.S. Landranger Sheet 202, map ref. 7069
Services: Post Office/village store, pub, tea room.
Nearest town: Ashburton.

Holne village stands as one of the gateways to the moor, situated some 200 metres above sea level, on the very edge of open moorland. To the south the view is of the soft, rolling hills of South Devon; to the north, a descent to the deep, wooded valley of the Dart, as it drops rapidly from the moor. The name for this area and village has developed from the Saxon *holle*, meaning 'deep valley'.

Holne is a small and attractive village, little changed in physical size since medieval days. Its population has been intertwined with life on the moor since Saxon times with the land and tin mining being its main preoccupations. The Church of St Mary is, as in many villages, the central pivot of the community, and stands solid against the predictable south westerly gale. Associated with the church and village are two well-known men from the past. Charles Kingsley, author of such classics as *Westward Ho!* was born at the Rectory in 1819. More than one hundred years later, the then Archbishop of Canterbury, Michael Ramsey, returned year after year to take his holiday at Holne, a tranquil haven after the affairs of church and state.

The Church House Inn

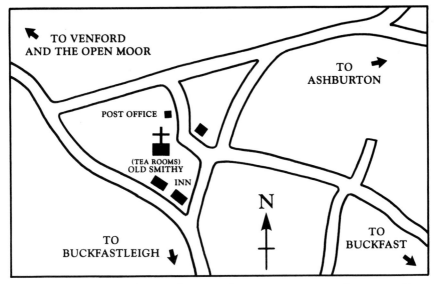

One can only wonder at how such men as these came to terms with certain village activities that were rather pagan in origin. For example 'The Holne Ram Feast' held in 'Play Field', saw the young men of the village catching the first ram they could find on the moor, and bringing it back to 'Play Field' where it was killed and roasted with great ceremony.

However, no doubt the power of both squire and vicar was considerable in days gone by; powerful enough to 'persuade' the blacksmith, being tempted every time he passed the Church House Inn on his way home, to take up new residence beside the smithy instead. (The smithy has since been converted into a charming tea room.)

As you enjoy a cream tea you can contemplate the fact that the same blacksmith, in addition to shoeing your horse, could also give you a quick haircut, thus making the most of his many skills, so necessary in an isolated community.

Should you leave the village on the Venford/Hexworthy road, as you drive through Moorgate out onto the open moor, spare a thought for the tin miners of Holne who had to trudge along this route, in all weathers, to the nearby mines. In the 1920's this particular piece of road was the first on Dartmoor to be tarmacked, bringing it well and truly into the 20th century.

Lustleigh

Situation: O.S. Landranger Sheet No. 191, map ref. 785814
Services: Post Office/store, dairy, tea rooms, select giftshop,
pub with accommodation.
Nearest town: Bovey Tracey.

The village of Lustleigh can be easily missed, lying as it does off the main Bovey Tracey/Moretonhampstead road, tucked in neatly amongst the foothills of Dartmoor. The name is probably better known in association with Lustleigh Cleave, a beauty spot situated to the west of the village.

The one drawback for the visitor, but one which has obviously helped to conserve the village's present identity, is a shortage of parking space.

The village has developed around the 13th century Church of St John the Baptist, which is in itself a building of considerable interest. Within the churchyard can be found another building worthy of attention - The Old Vestry. One presumes it was once used for this purpose but it was actually constructed in 1825 as the village school. Today it has a multitude of uses which reflect the active life of the village. The Parish Council hold their meetings here as do some of the fourteen local organisations, and it is also used as a surgery. Upstairs the village archives are lovingly cared for and added to by the local Historical Society. The exhibits are on view every Monday between 10 a.m. and midday.

The centre of the village has a cluster of 16th and 18th century buildings, including the village shops and pub. The village roots are indeed ancient and deep, with a mention in Doomsday as the only manor in Devon keeping bees for the production of honey; still obtainable today, throughout most of the year!

On the west side of the village, accessible down a cul-de-sac between dairy and Post Office, can be found 'The Town Orchard'. An area of 'semi-tamed land for the recreational use of the locals', it contains the granite throne, set up on a large granite boulder known as the 'Cleave' where the village May Queen is crowned on the first Saturday of that month.

In 1866 the opening of the Newton Abbot/Moretonhampstead railway line put Lustleigh on the map and made it very accessible to the Victorian day-tripper. Closed in 1958, the site of the old line still exists and seems to transect the village.

The village green, Lustleigh

In fact the settlement to the east of the line is called Wreyland, and was once a totally separate hamlet. It is a delight to walk along the footpath from Lustleigh green, passing under the old railway line and by the village cricket ground, to reach the picture-book thatched cottages of Wreyland, where the weathered skills of Victorian stone-masons, and the lack of car fumes contribute to a memorable experience. Wreyland was in fact the home of its own author, Cecil Torr, who wrote *Small Talk at Wreyland*, an insight into Devon village life with all its intrigues and gossip.

Radiating out from the village hub, Victorian, and later country residences, now cover the surrounding slopes, but with plenty of tree growth and 'sympathetic' gardening this later development blends in well.

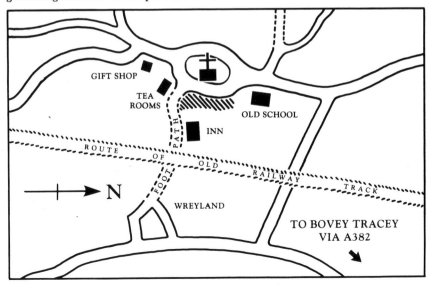

GIFT SHOP

TEA ROOMS

OLD SCHOOL

INN

FOOTPATH

ROUTE OF OLD RAILWAY TRACK

N

WREYLAND

TO BOVEY TRACEY VIA A382

Belstone

Situation: O.S. Landranger Sheet No.191, map ref. 619936
Services: Post Office, licensed restaurant, smithy.
Nearest town: Okehampton.

The village of Belstone stands on the very flanks of the open moor, some 300 metres above sea level. It is very much a working village and not out to attract or depend on the sightseer, with the exception of the passing walker on his or her way on or off the moor, or riders on their way to the local stables.

In this hard environment the overall characteristic is one of resilience, with little to soften a rugged exterior. The buildings - including the Church of St Mary the Virgin - are low and squat, protection against frequent gales and rain.

Even so, its character has appeal, with some specific points of interest for the visitor. The most noteworthy and attractive is the Post Office, housed in what was once a Zionist Chapel built in 1841. It has been a Post Office, or, as stated above the door, a telegraph office, for at least 70 years.

Towards the bottom of the village, on the south side of the road, can be found the village stocks, complete with granite seat. Very thoughtful! Slightly further up the hill, on the same side of the road, is the village 'pound'. Constructed to keep stray stock in, it now contains a small garden, for the pleasure of all, and is well protected from the Dartmoor breezes.

The village stocks, Belstone

Old Chapel & Telegraph office, now Post Office

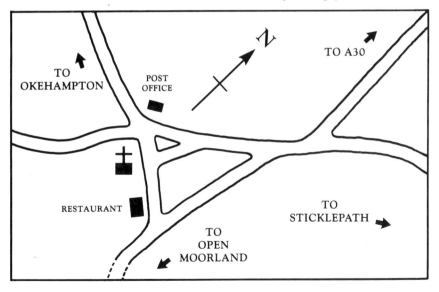

Postbridge

Situation: O.S. Landranger Sheet 191, map ref. 648790
Services: Post Office/village store/petrol pumps. Hotel/inn.
National Park Information Centre/Free Parking.
Excellent starting point for a range of walks.
Nearest town : Princetown.

Postbridge came into being to serve the Dartmoor traveller due to its stategic position as a crossing place over the East Dart. Originally a fording place, the developing trade in tin and wool during the 13th century saw a need to overcome the delays caused by the river when in flood and the now most visited 'clapper bridge' on Dartmoor was constructed. Forty-two feet long, by eight and a half feet high, constructed of four huge granite slabs supported on three piles, the bridge must have been of considerable benefit for the tinners and wool merchants en route between the stannary towns of Chagford and Tavistock.

As well as a river crossing Postbridge was a crossroads, with an important north/south track crossing the Chagford/Tavistock way here. However, it wasn't until the late 18th century that the village began to grow towards its present size and character. With the encouragement of the then Prince of Wales, together with people such as Thomas Tyrwhitt, areas of the moor were to be opened up to

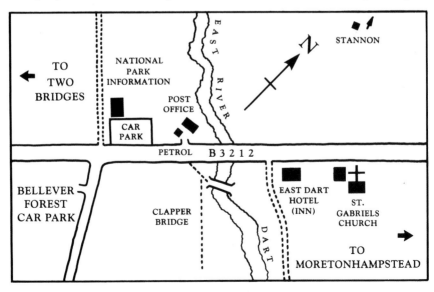

Postbridge(s)

both agricultural and industrial development. In the 1790's a turnpike road was built across the moor between Moretonhampstead and Tavistock with a new 'County' bridge - the present road bridge - built at Postbridge. A toll house and gate were positioned on the west side of the bridge, but these were demolished in 1863. A new local industry launched in those pioneering days was the production of starch from locally grown cereals at nearby Stannon House. Many of the beech trees seen in and around the village were planted at this time. The present village hostelry, The East Dart Hotel, is a relatively modern building. Before its construction the village 'Ale House' stood just behind the present site. Further up the road, away from the bridge, can be found the small village Church of St Gabriel. Built in 1868 it was simultaneously used as both a chapel of rest and a day school! At the turn of the century children attending school had to bring one piece of peat each day to fuel the fire.

A final symbol of Postbridge's part in the Dartmoor scene is Drift Lane, the route off the North Moor, following beside the west bank of the East Dart into the village and easily viewed from the Tourist Information car park. Drift Lane was used for driving stock down off the high moor over many centuries, and now for the intrepid Dartmoor walker, the view of Postbridge must have been, and is, a welcome haven from what can be wild moorland weather.

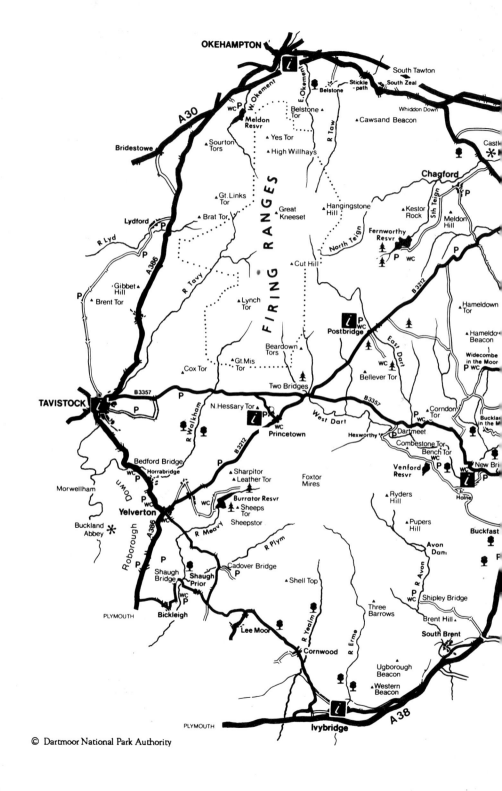

© Dartmoor National Park Authority

DARTMOOR

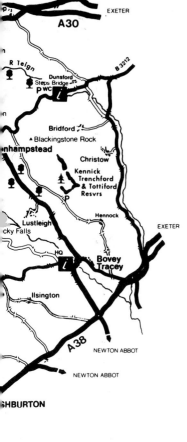

P⁻₁   EXETER

A30

R Telgn   B 3212

Dunsford
Steps Bridge
P WC   *i*

Bridford
▲ Blackingstone Rock

nhampstead

Christow

Kennick
Trenchford
& Tottiford
Resvrs

P

Hennock

Lustleigh   EXETER
cky Falls

HQ

i   Bovey
Tracey

Ilsington

A38

NEWTON ABBOT

NEWTON ABBOT

HBURTON

KEY	*i*	Dartmoor National Park Information Centre
	P Parking	**WC** Toilets

LEIGH

ES & TORBAY

2	3	4	5	miles

2	3	4	5	kilometres

North Bovey

Situation: O.S.Landranger Sheet 191, map ref. 740840
Services: Inn. Free car park opposite church.
Nearest town: Moretonhampstead.

North Bovey is one of those villages that, at first glance, seems frozen in time, except for the ever-present telephone cables and T.V. aerials. Situated around its village green the thatched cottages and church are a perfect example of 'the tranquil English village'. In fact, because it is situated in a backwater, on no specific route, it does not come to the attention of the majority of holiday visitors.

However, for those who like an uncommercial world for an hour or so it is well worth a visit. Pick your time well and the village pub, The Ring of Bells, whose structure and character merge perfectly into the village setting, will provide you with adequate refreshment. The Inn was originally a traditional Devonshire longhouse, with bakehouse attached and still visible.

The age of the majority of the village buildings is 15th and 16th century with the Church of St John the Baptist going back, in part, to the 13th century.

The population and services that once gave the village such a vigorous heart are now long gone. The fascination is in finding and mulling over the now-closed school house that had 65 children on roll only 30 years ago. Also the two village shops, now also sadly closed.

The village green is itself a place of fascination and interest. The present granite cross, although very old, replaced the original, destroyed during the Civil War. Also present are the village pump and a number of granite memorial stones celebrating such events as Queen Victoria's Jubilee. The chiming of the church clock as you look up towards the moor will complete a picture of a world now sadly past.

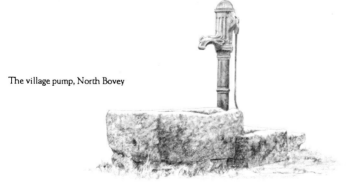

The village pump, North Bovey

The Church of St. John the Baptist, North Bovey

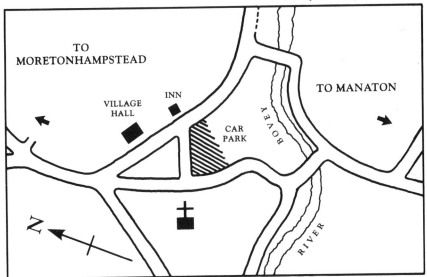

Lydford

Situation: O.S. Landranger Sheet No.191, map ref. 510848
Services: Post Office/shop, tea rooms, 2 pubs, garage, car park.
Nearest Town: Tavistock.

The village of Lydford has the honour of having been one of the four most important 'towns' in Devon. During the Saxon era, with the country experiencing attacks from the Danes, King Alfred made Lydford an administrative centre due to its good defensive site. With this function it was allowed to mint its own coins, samples of which can be seen in the Castle Arms Inn. Remains of the outer defensive bank can also still be seen running at right-angles away from the high street, just above (north-east) of the Post Office.

As time passed importance of one kind gave way to infamy of another. During the Middle Ages the tinners of Dartmoor were allowed to make their own laws and hold their own courts. This gave them considerable power over the local area and anyone involved in extracting tin. The original Norman castle at Lydford, built within the Saxon town area, was redeveloped as a prison for anyone breaking the tinners' laws. The present 'castle' is the ruin of that prison. From what we are told

Lydford Castle and the Castle Inn

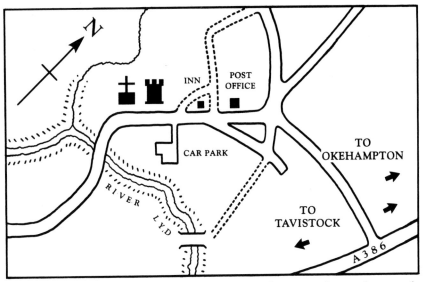

the innocent often paid the same price as the guilty, very often without trial. As the saying goes:

I oft have heard of Lydford law
How in the morn they hang and draw
And sit in judgement after.

Beside this gruesome place stands the 15th century Church of St Petrock, a beautiful and suitable counterweight to its evil but interesting neighbour.

In early medieval days the church at Lydford was the centre of a moorland parish of over 50,000 acres, and remains today the largest parish in Devon. In those early days anyone dying in the Parish had to be buried at Lydford. Across the moor there are various paths called 'Lich (or Lych) Ways'. These originated as routes for carrying the dead to Lydford for burial and were often of considerable length.

At the lower (south westerly) end of the village the hillside drops precipitously into Lydford Gorge and the River Lyd. It was this dramatic and beautiful natural feature that helped to make 'the town' such a defensible position in Saxon days. A walk along the gorge, now owned by the National Trust, is very worthwhile. Today Lydford is a small, sleepy Devonshire village, a long way removed from its Royal birth over one thousand years ago. Not for it the submergence under centuries of development, rather a bypassing of time, with a subtle wielding of influence over a moorland kingdom.

Buckland-in-the-Moor

Situation: O.S.Landranger Sheet 191, map ref.720730
Services: Craft shop/Tea rooms.
Nearest town: Ashburton.

A very small, picturesque village situated on the west facing, lower slopes of the moor, overlooking the Dart Valley and its tributary, the Webburn.

Although probably the site of a Saxon farmstead the name first appears in recorded form when Roger de Bokelonde gave the manor as a gift to the monks of Tor Abbey in the mid 13th century. This was in gratitude for his safe return from the Crusades. *Bokelonde* means 'the bookland' or land as detailed in a charter.

The village Church of St Peter, to be found at the top end of the village on the Widecombe road, is many centuries old with some original 12th century stonework still visible. It is a beautiful structure, its squat, grey granite form now as much a part of the landscape as the natural tors on the surrounding moors.

Today this church is probably best known for its unusual clock, to be found on the east side of the tower, facing the road. Instead of numbers there are letters making up the words 'MY DEAR MOTHER'. This clock face was donated in 1930 by William Whitley, the then 'Lord of the Manor', as a memorial to his mother.

Turning down beside the church is a steep, narrow, lane which leads the adventurous walker or driver into a woodland in which Grimm's characters would have felt at home. This lane and its surrounding beauty drops you quickly to the Dart and its confluence with the Webburn.

Should you ignore this route for the time being and continue on down the road towards the centre of the village you will pass Buckland Court on your right. This Georgian house was the family seat of the Bastard family, lords of the manor for many generations. The road, especially in summertime, seems to burrow

The tower of St Peter's Church, Buckland-in-the- Moor

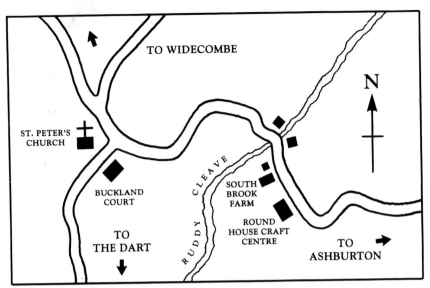

through luxurious vegetation, bordered on either side by walls covered thickly in moss and lichen. Set in this roadside wall, adjacent to Buckland Court, can be found an old medieval cross, if searched for diligently. The centre of the village consists of a cluster of granite and thatched cottages, together with what was once the school and the Post Office. They are situated on both sides of a fast-flowing brook, the Ruddycleave; no doubt named after the peaty colour of the water. Having filled a well-used horse trough, the stream passes under the road and on down the valley. This idyllic scene has graced many a chocolate box lid and the solitude, found more often out of season, appeals even to wintering herons who can be seen hunting for fish with enviable patience.

However, the scene is not always one of tranquillity. In 1939 the Ruddycleave brook became a destructive torrent and both cottage and bridge were carried away. Just up the road, on the opposite side, is Southbrook Farm, originally a manor court and of considerable importance to the local community. Adjoining the farm is the horse wheel barn, constructed in the last century to provide the farmer with an additional means of grinding corn. Today it has been converted into a craft centre and tearoom but it still retains the historical character of the area.

To the east of the village the hillside rises up onto the open moorland of Buckland Common. On the skyline, and visible from the church and other vantage points, you can see Buckland Beacon. Used as a signal point for centuries past, the Beacon, or tor, is well worth a visit, not only for the views that can be enjoyed from its summit, but also to inspect the 'Ten Commandments' cut into two slabs of granite in 1928 on the instruction of William Whitley.

Poundsgate

Situation: O.S. Landranger Sheet 191, map ref. 7072
Services: Post Office/village Store, pub, garage/petrol.
Nearest Town: Ashburton.

The village of Poundsgate could really be classified as a hamlet, yet it provides more for the local and visitor than many larger villages.

Like its neighbours Holne and Buckland, Poundsgate is set high up, 200 metres above sea level. It is impossible to miss the village as it is situated on either side of the main Ashburton/Two Bridges road, the A384. Although a major route across the moor, the narrow bridges across the Dart limit the amount of heavy traffic. After the steep climb up from New Bridge the village is a pleasant stopping place, especially on a sunny spring or autumn day.

The centre of the village, and the most conspicuous building, is the pub, the Tavistock Inn. Its most famous visitor is said to have been the devil, who called in with fiery breath to quench his thirst before continuing on his way to perform his destructive and deadly work at Widecombe on Sunday 21st October 1638. Today the Inn is a popular meeting place particularly during the summer months when it is renowned for its spectacular hanging baskets.

Further down the road towards Two Bridges, on the left, can be seen a traditionally constructed and picturesque granite cottage. Recently renovated, this building is thought to be originally 17th century, and was once the Post Office, complete with original telephone exchange for the Spitchwick/Holne area. Next door was once the village bakery and opposite was the smithy, with the mounting block still in place at the side of the building.

As you climb out of the village around a steep, tight hairpin bend, a small 'pound' or enclosure can be seen at the side of the road, on the left. This is the pound which has given the village its name. Used for enclosing stray stock, it still has some use today.

Further on up the hill and then to the right, can be found Leusdon Church. Set in glorious isolation, overlooking the Webburn and Dart, this small country church serves Poundsgate and the other hamlets and farmsteads of Spitchwick.

The Tavistock Inn

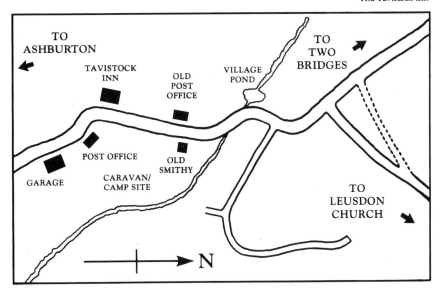

Manaton

Situation: O.S. Landranger Sheet 191, map ref. 750813
Services: Post Office/village stores. pub.
Nearest Town: Moretonhamstead.

Manaton village is the centre of one of Dartmoor's largest parishes and the village, although sparsely populated, is spread over a considerable area. It is, in fact, divided into three parts, all lying off the B3344 Bovey Tracey road. The original village centre nestles beside its 15th century mother Church of St Winifred, with village green and separate village cricket pitch in close proximity.

A third of a mile down the road towards Bovey are the other two parts of the village, once the evocatively named, independent hamlets of Freeland and Water, now all part of Manaton. As one drives along the road, the Post Office and Kestor Inn (headquarters of the M.C.C!) are clearly seen, but the more picturesque parts

Water, Manaton

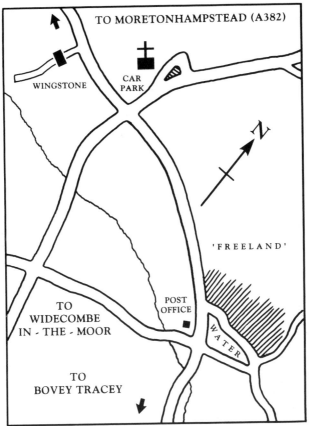

of Freeland and Water are not. A brief stop here, and time to amble along the narrow lane to the east of the road, enables you to experience a combination of weathered thatched cottages set in granite, lush vegetation and dancing water; a harmonious blend of man and nature. Water, as you might imagine, is the ideal site for a mill and indeed, there it still stands, but now a private residence.

The stimulation of the beautiful surroundings and the local populace were obviously an important factor in encouraging the poet John Galsworthy to make his home here at 'Wingstone', close by the church.

Ponder awhile and no doubt you will understand why.

Sticklepath

Situation: O.S. Landranger Sheet No.191, map ref. 640940
Services: Post Office, village store, 2 inns, garage/car hire.
Nearest Town: Okehampton.

The village of Sticklepath owes its existence to its position on what was once a major trade route between Exeter and Launceston, and to trades associated with the industrial revolution. As such, its background, buildings and character are not dissimilar to certain villages in the Midlands and South Wales, although of course those industrial days are long gone.

Up to the mid 1980's, Sticklepath's life was inextricably bound to the main Exeter/Okehampton trunk road - the dreaded A30 - with heavy traffic thundering incessantly through the village. But the construction of the new dual-carriageway has meant that, for the first time in its existence, the village has become a backwater, no longer on a main artery of commercial life.

Three hundred years ago the A30 was no more than a track, but it brought life to the area. It was along this track, where it fell steeply down the hillside to the River Taw, that the village developed. 'Stickle' in fact means 'steep' and referred to the steep track descending, or climbing, 'The Mount' before the present road was built taking a more gentle route. The Mount is the conspicuous hill at the western (Okehampton) end of the village.

Although a small hamlet was probably here in Saxon and Norman times, it was the industrial revolution and the need for a source of power, close at hand, that saw Sticklepath blossom. Water from the River Taw, pouring off the moor, was to turn at least seven water wheels and thereby drive a multitude of machines, from bellows to hammers. A leat was taken from the river at the base of The Mount, along the backs of the various mills and works, parallel with the main street, and then back into the river.

During the 18th and 19th centuries, Sticklepath's proximity to the tin and copper mines of Devon and Cornwall, and the local copper mines of Ramsley and Greenhill, provided a ready market for a whole range of mining equipment.

Today, a part living reminder of the past industry of this little place can be seen and experienced in the Finch Foundry Museum. The original foundry, complete

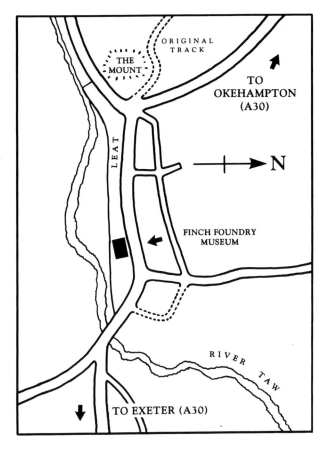

with water wheel, launders and working machinery, remains in being and is currently being renovated to give an accurate example of the power of water and the skills of our predecessors.

The people who had settled and made their homes in Sticklepath had much in common with other similar mining and industrial communities. The road very much played its part in bringing strangers, views and news at a time when communications were often lacking. It was the road that brought the Quaker religion to Sticklepath during the reign of Charles II, with the influx of a Quaker community of 200 people. A century later it was the road that brought John Wesley through the village. It is said that in response to local demand, he preached to the villagers on The Mount, where a white flagpole now stands. From then on the local community became very much a Methodist stronghold.

Sticklepath is also a well known name in geological circles as one of the longest fault lines in the West Country runs through the village and is named after it. Over millions of years the land has moved in opposite directions along either side of the fault. How many of the millions of travellers who have passed along this road will have known that the ground that contains the old mine workings at Ramsley, and that at Greenhill, were once adjoining? Today they are one mile apart!

Who would have thought that such examples of power and movement, both physical and spiritual, could be found in what is now such a peaceful backwater?

The now tranquil high street of Sticklepath, once the main route from Exeter to North Devon

Sheepstor

Situation: O.S.Landranger Sheet No.202, map ref. 560677
Services: None.
Nearest Town: Yelverton.

Sheepstor is another small Dartmoor settlement serving a population over a large area, although much of that area now lies under the waters of the Burrator Reservoir. Before the building of the reservoir, which supplies Plymouth, the area was much involved with mining and agriculture.

For the people living within this parish, the church at Sheepstor was where they would come on a regular basis. The hamlet - which takes its name from the mighty tor standing protectively to the north - seems to be an extension of the same natural phenomenon, with its narrow lanes, lichen-covered and granite-lined, and the church itself, spilling to the valley floor to lie exposed to the elements, without the dressing of abundant foliage usually found in similar settings.

The church and its surrounding cottages, clustered tightly together, provide a peaceful haven from the seasonal bustle beside the Burrator dam. This tranquil church is an apt resting place for two members of the Brooke family, once owners of a local estate, as well as being 'Rajahs of Sarawak' during the 19th and early 20th

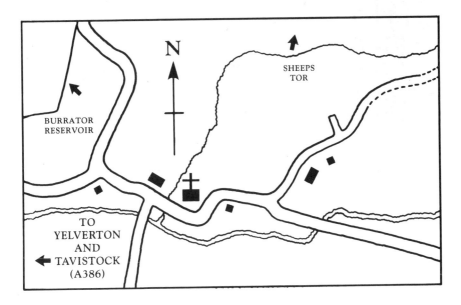

centuries. Inside the church there is a large commemorative plaque which describes in detail the long-term unselfish service the family gave to Sarawak and its people, all those thousands of miles away.

Sheepstor village